Created by
"Jokin'" Jim Davis

Written by
"Madcap" Mark Acey and
"Snickerin'" Scott Nickel

Designed by
"Kooky" Kenny Goetzinger

Illustrated by
"Mirthful" Mike Fentz and
"Loony" Lori Barker

A Ballantine Book
Published by The Random House Ballantine Publishing Group
Copyright © 2003 by PAWS, Inc. All Rights Reserved.

www.ballantinebooks.com

ISBN 0-345-46263-7

Manufactured in the United States of America

First Edition: May 2003

10 9 8 7 6 5 4 3 2 1

GARFIELD'S Joke Zone

Here's Garfield!

Why did Garfield cross the road?

To get to the pizza parlor on the other side!

What's Garfield's favorite kind of book?

A cookbook!

If Garfield were a vegetable, what kind would he be?

A *couch potato!*

What kind of music do mummies like?

Wrap music!

Knock, knock.
Who's there?
Harry.
Harry who?
Harry up and open the door!

Why does Garfield like computers?

Because he can play with the mouse, but he doesn't have to eat it!

What would you get if you crossed a basketball player with a famous escape artist?

Hoopdini!

Where do vampires keep their money?

In a blood bank!

What's 100 feet tall, orange, and eats its way through Japan?

Garzilla!

Class Clowning

What did the space alien get for his school report?

Extraterrestrial credit!

What kind of books do librarians hate?

Overdue books!

What do you call a pirate who always skips school?

Captain Hooky!

Why did the chicken stop playing baseball?

It kept hitting fowl balls!

Who's orange and furry and doesn't like Toto?

The Wizard of Paws!

Knock, knock!

Who's there?

Jackie-Anne.

Jackie-Anne who?

Jackie-Anne Jilly
went up the hilly.

Why did Odie bring Jon a pair of bananas?

Because Jon asked Odie to fetch his slippers!

What would you get if you crossed a bear with a skunk?

Winnie the Pew!

How do cows count?

They use cowculators!

What dessert does Garfield eat in bed?

A sheet cake!

What do frogs drink?

Croaka-Cola!

What happens to Garfield when he eats a lemon?

He becomes a sourpuss!

What would you get if you crossed a pig with a map?

Ge-hog-raphy!

What do you call an egg from outer space?

An unidentified flying omelet!

On what day does Garfield cook hamburgers?

Fry-day!

Knock, knock.

Who's there?

Bacon.

Bacon who?

Bacon cookies just for you!

Who has webbed feet and fights crime?

Duck Tracy!

What would you get if you crossed Garfield with Quasimodo?

The Munchcat of Notre Dame!

What's tall, hairy, and goes, "Oink, oink"?

Pigfoot!

What would you get if you crossed a flying boy with a bear?

Peter Panda!

What happened to the chicken that stayed in the sun all day?

It got fried!

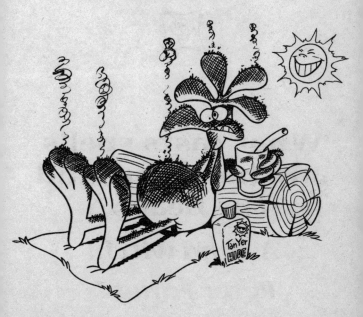

**Why did the firefly
skip a grade?**

He was very bright!

**What casts spells
and hangs around
the beach?**

A sand witch!

What does Garfield eat when he's grouchy?

Crabmeat!

Knock, knock!

Who's there?

Feline.

Feline who?

Feline blue because you won't let me in!

What do you call a boring toy?

A dull doll!

How did Garfield make the skeleton laugh?

He tickled his funny bone!

Where do baseball players eat?

Home plate!

What are the most athletic rodents?

Track and field mice!

Why doesn't Garfield play basketball?

He shoots too many hair balls!

**What famous
Viking loved books?**
Eric the Read!

Knock, knock.
Who's there?
York.
York who?
*York cat just
ate my bird!*

What's Garfield's favorite sport?

Mice hockey!

Cartoon Crack-Ups

What would you get if you crossed a cartoon dog with a cow?

Scooby-Moo!

What would you get if you crossed a smarter-than-average bear with a rabbit?

Yogi Hare!

Where does Superman shop for food?

At the supermarket, of course!

What would you get if you crossed a hamburger with a football player?

A Quarter Pounder Back!

What would you get if you crossed Nermal with a glove?

The world's cutest mitten!

**Where did Odie
sleep when he
went camping?**

In a pup tent!

What would you get if you crossed a cow with a red-nosed reindeer?

Moo-dolph!

What would you get if you crossed a cucumber with a kids' TV network?

Pickelodeon!

What's just as big as Garfield but doesn't weigh a single pound?

Garfield's shadow!

That's Entertainment

Who really did Babe the pig's dangerous movie scenes?

A stunt ham!

What would you get if you crossed a Jedi knight with a toad?

Star Warts!

What kind of music do mountain climbers like?

Rock music!

Knock, knock!
Who's there?
Ben.
Ben who?
Ben there. Done that.

**What's nice,
flies through walls,
and eats tin cans?**

*Casper the
Friendly Goat!*

What's Garfield's favorite fairy tale?

Beauty and the Feast!

What did Attila use at the beach?

Huntan lotion!

What did the mad doctor get when he crossed a skunk with his monster?

Stinkenstein!

What are the two things Garfield can never eat for breakfast?

Lunch and dinner!

Compute This!

What would you get if you crossed a computer with the family dog?

An Internet pet!

What do you call Rollerbladers who chat on the computer?

Online skaters!

Why did the spider like computers?

Because he had his own Web site!

What does a shark eat with peanut butter?

Jellyfish!

What kind of band can't play music?

A rubber band!

How does Odie
feel about winter?

It leaves him cold!

Knock, knock.
Who's there?
G. I.
G. I. who?
G. I. wish you'd
open the door!

Knock, knock.
Who's there?
Turnip.
Turnip, who?
Turnip the radio,
my favorite song
is playing!

If Garfield had ten donuts in one paw and nine donuts in the other, what would he have?

Big paws!

Loony Letters

What two letters describe Odie's head?

MT

What two letters describe a slippery street?

IC

What two letters does Garfield most like to watch?

TV

What would you get if you crossed an athlete with a Halloween pumpkin?

A jock-o'-lantern!

What kind of cookies do birds like?

Chocolate-chirp cookies!

What would you get if you crossed a dinosaur with a pig?

Jurassic pork!

Where do polar bears keep their money?

In snowbanks!

Knock, knock!
Who's there?
Freddy.
Freddy who?
*Freddy or not,
here I come!*

What's a monster's favorite snack?

Ghoul Scout cookies!

Jest for Laughs

What would you get if you crossed an automobile with a water park?

A carpool!

Why did the spy stay in bed all day?

He was working undercover!

**Why did Jon
take a broom to
the dance?**

*So he could sweep the
girls off their feet!*

What do you call a croaking pig?

Kermit the Hog!

What do you get when a dinosaur walks through a vegetable garden?

Squash!

Knock, knock!

Who's there?

Drew.

Drew who?

Drew a picture of Garfield and Odie!

57

What kind of cake do mice like?

Cheesecake!

What did the sad ghost say to Garfield?

Boo-hoo!

What is a witch's favorite subject?

Spell-ing!

Scared Silly

Did you hear about the TV show with FBI agents and witches?

It's called "The Hex-Files"!

What do spooks eat for dinner?

Ghost beef!

What would you get if you crossed Dracula with Odie?

A vampire who slobbers on your neck!

What does Odie do when it rains?

He gets wet!

Which insect is the smartest?

The bookworm!

Knock, knock!

Who's there?

Anita.

Anita who?

Anita more food—
here comes Garfield!

What do you call a kitten that does somersaults in the air?

An acrocat!

What Old West outlaw had ten arms?

Billy the Squid!

Why did Garfield wear sneakers?

So he could sneak up on Odie!

Knutty Knock-Knocks

Knock, knock!
Who's there?
Dragon.
Dragon who?
Dragon this big tail around makes me tired!

Nice haircut.
Still going to
the dog groomer?

KNOCKOUTS!

Knock, knock.
Who's there?
Ima.
Ima who?
Ima lot smarter than you!

Knock, knock!
Who's there?
Kareem.
Kareem who?
Kareem-filled cupcakes are Garfield's favorite!

What would you get if you crossed an icy villain with a tiny bug?

Mr. Fleas!

Why did Garfield swat the fly?

It was bugging him!

Who swings from a vine and cannot tell a lie?

George Washington of the Jungle!

What did King Arthur sleep with when he was afraid of the dark?

A knight-light!

What is a ghost's favorite breakfast food?

Boo-berry muffins!

Why isn't Odie good at basketball?

Because he can drool, but he can't dribble!

What Can It Be?

**What has teeth
but can't bite?**

A comb!

**What has three
feet but can't walk?**

A yard!

What can Garfield take but not give back?

A nap!

What would you get if you crossed a frog with a squirt gun?

A Croaker Soaker!

What is Garfield's least favorite cake?

A cake of soap!

What's the difference between a dog and a flea?

A dog can have fleas, but a flea can't have dogs!

What would you get if you crossed baseball with a space movie?

The Umpire Strikes Back!

What did the little cob call its father?

Pop Corn!

What did Garfield say after he kicked Odie off the table?

"Doggone!"

Did you hear the
one about the
werewolf?

It's a howler!

Did you hear the
one about the
spaceship?

It's out of this world!

Did you hear the one about the teacher?

It's in a class by itself!

What did the coach tell the upset wrestler?

"Get a grip!"

What do birds say on Halloween?

"Trick or tweet?"

Why was the noisy dog removed from the street?

He was in a "no barking" zone!

Where do trains race?

At track meets!

What would you get if you crossed Odie with a deer?

Dumbi!

What is Garfield's favorite type of story?

A furry tale!

What would you call a surprise test about Odie?

A pup quiz!

What state is home to Lassie the dog?

Collie-fornia!

What do you call Odie after Garfield sprays him with water?

A soggy doggy!

What spider makes the best father?

A daddy longlegs!

Did you hear the one about the red pepper?

It's hot stuff!

What would you get if you crossed a duck with the Fourth of July?

A fire quacker!

Why did the boy take his dirty laundry to the magician?

He wanted the stains to disappear!

What flavor of ice cream do monsters like best?

Cookies and scream!

How did Vikings communicate?

They used Norse code!

Where do genies go on summer vacation?

To lamp camp!

What's the tallest building in Transylvania?

The Vampire State Building!

How do you drive Odie crazy?

Put him in a round room and tell him to go stand in the corner!

Knock, knock!

Who's there?

Roach.

Roach who?

*Roach you a letter
but you didn't answer.*

Knock, knock!
Who's there?
Carrie.
Carrie who?
Carrie Garfield?!
He's way too heavy!

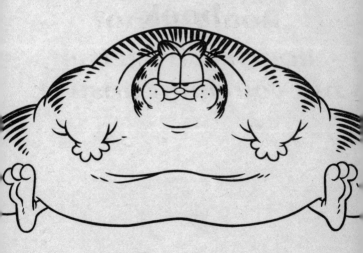

**Flip
book
over**

Created by
Jim *"Diss This!"* Davis

Written by
Mark *"In Your Facey"* Acey
Scott *"The Snot"* Nickel

Designed by
Kenny *"Too Cool to Care"* Goetzinger

Illustrated by
Mike *"Mad Dog"* Fentz
Glenn *"Bad Dog"* Zimmerman
Larry *"Lap Dog"* Fentz
Lori *"Pit Bull"* Barker

GARFIELD'S

IN-YOUR-FACE INSULTS

Know what
goes best with
a face like yours?
A paper bag.

Nice hair.
Still styling it with
a Weedwacker?

Want to fight air pollution? Then keep your shoes on!

"Brain" is your middle name. "Lame" is your first.

Heard you got a brain transplant, and the ox's brain rejected *you*.

You're so stupid,
you flunked recess!

When it comes to being ugly...you're an overachiever!

Looks aren't everything. In your case, they're *nothing*!

Is that your face, or did your pants fall down?

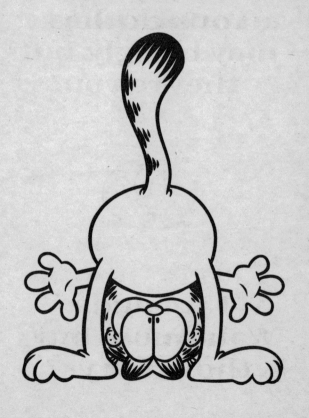

DRESSED TO ILL

Your clothes
may be ugly, but
they're you.

Nice duds.
Your mom buy
those for ya?

I had a shirt just like that after the dog barfed on it.

I love your teeth. Green is your color.

Are those braces, or are your teeth under arrest?

I've seen nicer teeth
in my comb!

You're about as
much fun as
summer school
in the Sahara!

You're so boring,
your Web site is
dullerthandirt.com!

You're as popular as an elephant with a runny nose!

CRAZY CURSES

May you floss a pit bull!

May you get a zit the size of a kumquat!

May your tongue grow fur!

I've seen better looking hair in the shower drain!

Your hair's so greasy, you can fry chicken in it!

Is that your hair, or did a porcupine climb up on your head and die?

Where'd you get those big feet? From a Clydesdale?

If your feet were any bigger, they'd be yards!

Where do you shop for shoes? Clowns "R" Us?

SNAPPY COMEBACKS

Did you do your homework?

No, the dog did it
for me.

No, I'm trying to
kick the habit.

No, the TV wouldn't
let me.

Where are your manners?

I left them in my locker.

I dunno. I thought
you had them.

I gave them the day off.

It's time to get up!

I just got up yesterday.

Tell morning
to come back later.

Call my school...
tell them I died.

Are you always this dorky, or is today a special occasion?

You're like a breath of stale air.

You're about as graceful as a rhino on Rollerblades!

I'd love to stay
and talk, but I'm
missing the
Weather Channel.

Are those clothes
for real, or are you
trick-or-treating
as an Easter egg?

Are those your skinny legs, or are you riding a flamingo?

GEEK CHIC

Hey, I hear you
made the cover of
Dorks Illustrated!

You're so nerdy,
you make
Mr. Rogers
look cool!

You're no ordinary geek. You're Geekzilla!

You're as irritating
as a hungry horde
of chiggers!

I've seen
belly-button lint
with more brains
than you!

**You smell like
a sweaty sumo
wrestler's armpit!**

You can't count to twenty without taking your shoes off!

Your family tree is full of nuts!

You're about as graceful as a buffalo on a balance beam!

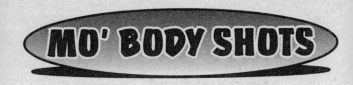

MO' BODY SHOTS

You have the
perfect face...
for a dartboard!

The only thing
that smells worse
than your feet is
your breath!

You're like Odie. You've got a soft heart... and a head to match!

**You're so dumb,
you think the
toilet bowl is a
football game.**

**Know what I like
about your looks?
Nothing!**

I've seen wolverines with nicer smiles.

You're so dumb,
your mom
serves you
"pea brain" soup.

You look
pretty good...
for roadkill.

Is that your mouth or the Grand Canyon?

JOB JABS

Teachers:

"I wish *I* only had to work nine months out of the year."

Clowns:

"If I had your job, I wouldn't show my real face either."

Veterinarians:

"At least when you mess up, it's only on some dumb animal."

**You've got ears
like a famous
movie star...
Mickey Mouse!**

**Last time I saw
a nose like yours,
it had an elephant
attached to it!**

You're two-faced.
And they're
both ugly!

You smell as funky as a monkey!

You'd have to study just to be stupid.

You have a memory
like an elephant.
And a figure
like one, too.

You're so dumb...
you think a
baby-sitter sits
on babies!

You're so dumb...
you once tried to
feed cheese to your
computer's mouse.

You're so dumb... you think toothpaste is for loose teeth!

You smell like an acre of wet dogs!

You look like you've been whupped with the ugly stick.

You've got the IQ of a turnip!

You only bore me on days ending in *y*.

You look like a visitor from the planet Geeko.

**Next time you're
out shopping,
buy yourself
a personality.**

You're so fat,
you have a
quadruple chin!

You're so fat,
when you were
born, your first
word was "Oink"!

You're so fat, you could be Shamu's stunt double.

If you were smarter, you'd know how dumb you are!

You're a total zero. In fact, you might even be a minus one.

Your clothes always attract attention. Not to mention flies.

With your looks you could win a prize... at a dog show!

You're so short, you need a ladder to reach the curb.

Your breath is so bad, even a skunk won't kiss you!

Why don't you exercise more?

More than what?

Oh, no! The "E" word!

Why don't you annoy me less?

Do you have the time?

Yes, and I'm going to keep it.

Yes, but I don't have the patience to talk to a dipwad like you.

Time for what? More of your stupid questions?

What happened to your allowance?

I lost it in the stock market.

The Tooth Fairy was broke, so I loaned it to him.

My evil twin blew it on a nose ring.

Know what two letters describe your breath?

PU!

You don't need to brush your teeth. You need to sandblast them!

You've got enough wax in your ears to start your own candle company!

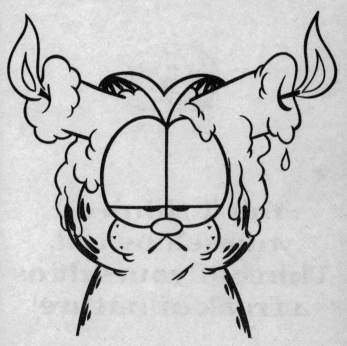

Your ears aren't big...for a basset hound!

Don't think of yourself as tall. Think of yourself as a freak of nature!

**Your legs look
like a turkey's on
the day after
Thanksgiving!**

EVEN MO' BODY SHOTS

Is that your new 'do, or did your cat hack up a hairball on your head?

Your feet could out-stink a gym locker!

Knock, knock.
Who's there?
Hugh.
Hugh who?
Hugh smell.

Take your face to outer space!

Don't ever change. I want to forget you just the way you are.

**I'll miss you like
I'll miss poison ivy.**

You're as interesting as a documentary on dirt!

"Exciting" is your middle name. "Un" is your first!

You're as lively as a comatose librarian!

QUIET!

IN THE DOGHOUSE

I've seen
stuffed animals
with more brains
than your dog!

Your dog's a rare
breed: 100% ugly!

Your dog is so fat, you can't take him for a walk... you take him for a waddle!

**Hey, hippo hips!
Bust any toilet
seats lately?**

**You don't need
a bib. You need
a tarp!**

The only thing bigger than your stomach is your appetite!

**You have a
striking face.
So who's been
striking it?**

**Be it ever
so homely, there's
no face like yours!**

A face like yours belongs in the movies... horror movies!

SON OF CRAZY CURSES

May a family of rabid squirrels build a nest in your head!

May a dopey dog drool on your homework!

May mutant leftovers breed in your refrigerator!

You're not as dumb as you look. But who could be?!

Your IQ is so low you can't measure it... you have to dig for it.

If space aliens captured you, they'd report no intelligent life on Earth!

Make like a tree and leave!

Make like a dog and get lost!

Make like a banana and split!

DARTS TO THE HEART

Sorry, I don't date lower life-forms.

You've made this a date I won't forget... no matter how hard I try.

Kiss you?
I'd rather kiss an
orangutan with
a cold sore!

**Last time I saw
a noggin like
yours was on
Mr. Potato Head!**

**How can
such a humongous
head hold such a
puny brain?**

Is that your head
or a hotel for lice?

**You should try
doing something
new with your hair.
Like washing it.**

**Know what
goes great with a
body like yours?
A barf bag!**

Nice look...
for a court jester!

There's a bus leaving at three. Be under it!

You're a person of rare intelligence. It's rare when you show any!

If you were any shorter, you could date Barbie!

UGLY IS AS UGLY DOES

Your family's
so ugly, their gene
pool needs a
bucket of chlorine.

You're so ugly,
even a garbage
collector wouldn't
take you out!

You're so ugly, when you look in a mirror, your reflection throws up!

**Flip
book
over**